We Are Forever
Awaken With Poetry

Cheryl Lunar Wind
Cody Ray Richardson

We Are Forever

Awaken With Poetry

Some of the poems in this collection first appeared in Life: Shared thru Poetry, Know Your Way, We Are One, Follow the White Rabbit and Love Your Light chapbooks; and on facebook.

Cover credit, painting by Cody Ray Richardson.

First edition.

Published by Four Wild Geese Design, Mount Shasta, California 96067

ISBN 978-1-7324373-8-8

Dedicated to all those
beautiful souls
learning, growing and loving.

Preface

"Sometimes, our minds need a round-about way to get there."

I never realized what an important role the Arts(songs, poetry, plays, visual arts, ect.)would play in the awakening of humanity. We have Rumi, Shakespeare's lessons, the Psalms, Solomon's wisdom, Jesus' parables and all the ancient stories from many different tribes. I would like to add Mount Shasta poetry to the list. This is Cody Ray Richardson's first book of inspirational poetry, and I am excited to see more.

A friend once told me that we all have at least one book inside of us.

Raise your words
not your voice...RUMI

"So let your love free to the wind
There is no holding on
What's meant to stay will never go away
It will always be where it belongs."
--Cody Ray Richardson

Contents

Freedom by Cheryl

The three sisters
named the game
Fate.

Dive off a steep reef--
Meet a herd of dolphin.
Be a friend, not foe.

Hope to climb back up--
Toad on a sugarcane stalk.

Toads and pixies play together.
Ring around the posy.

Daisies grow best in sandy soil.

A mage,
better known as the wiz--
plays a jute
while nude
girls, girls, girls
are ready for fun.

Slaves make speedy escape--
while a woolly dog wanders in fog,
no longer guarding the crew--

Mutiny. Run away. Exodus.

No more daily grind--
Put away your mop and broom.

Eagles fly free.

Trial of the century--
Pivotal day in court.
Human beings
Set free.

Changing of the Seasons by Cody

Changing of the seasons.
Emotions of nature.
Drought to dust.
Flood it out.
Freeze it to stagnation.
Melt it all away.
Throw it rapidly down a river.
Tears of the world.
Emotions gather in her teary eyes.
Lakes floating in the sky.
Fall on me, wash it all away.
Refreshed for another day.
Ride the changes like a wave.
Deep underground something stirs.
Feeding the creepy crawlers and the worms.
Seems so strange when the sun goes down.
Nothing left to loose.
Then the wind blows and tears away your blanket.
Dunes change shape.
Erosion of emotion.
Sifting through to find the Diamond.
Shifting until your on an island.
Will our hands touch?
Closer to our hearts?
Or will we be pulled away?
Further apart.

What is Your Weather Like?
by Cheryl

Mother Earth's
  Clean up team---

Wind, Rain and Snow
Wiping the slate clean.

Rein in your anger--
Rain.

Shout---
Pelt like hail.
Let it all out---

Release the dam you've built.
Flood--
of tears.

Blow like a blizzard.
The whistling wind
clears the way.

Nature shows us how.

I See You by Cody

I see you
You see me
Infinite Connection
Trapped in English Alchemy

Tiny Bowl by Cheryl & Giovanna

Background sounds bring life to food.
Good company, place to be free.
A tiny bowl filled with compassion--
Washes away a yearning heart.

Good company, place to be free.
Flowing, Cleansing heart and soul.
Washes away a yearning heart.
Longing to be loved and free.

Flowing, Cleansing heart and soul.
Holding space for all to heal.
Longing to be loved and free.
I see you and you see me.

Holding space for all to heal.
A tiny bowl filled with compassion--
I see you and you see me.
Background sounds bring life to food.

Gates, Keys, Acceptance and Forgiveness
by Cody

Come one Come all
The gates are open
You yourselves hold the keys
All seen and un seen
All guests and residents
No rituals required
No offerings needed
Acceptance and forgiveness
Are yours to converge
The son and daughter of creation and created
Allow yourself through
you are welcomed to paradise with open arms
Forgiveness will allow you to unload your
baggage
Acceptance will allow you to be as you are
A beautiful radiant internal light being
I see you
I love you

The Event by Cheryl

I want to tell you about a gathering.

It is a Cosmic happening.

Some call it the Event.
It has been planned long in advance.

All are invited----
the ancients, the innocents---even those viewed
as guilty.

Our acceptance gives us admittance.
Our knowing is the ticket.
The practice of peace will be our map.

The Cosmic Rays show us the way,   a cipher,
they light up the path.

Sacred codes are hidden like Easter eggs.
We find them all over---
In nature, on our clocks and in our dreams.
We create them in music and art.

Our family are waiting for us---
they hail from far and near.
The sacred Earth clans are present---
tree, crystal, bird, wolf, bear and deer tribes,
AND
Those who have traveled a millennium to be present.
All are here---

The Divine Director pulls the curtain,
It is a beautiful scene,
Glorious light fills the room.

Only You Can Show the World Who You Are
by Cody

All the faces I wear
The sad one
The glad one
The happy one
Mad one

That far off stare
You can be a winner that wins
You can be a loser that looses
You can even be a loser that wins
You are you from end to begin

Oh that place where
On your way to that 10
You might have to go through 9 1s
you might be number 9 for them
Then dumped for their 10

Here we are, there
The place we always are
Living in a mansion
Or living in a car
Near our destination
Far from our home star

Remember it's a journey
A destination unknown
Are you an actor
Or a musician
Only you can show the world who you are

Camp of Humanity by Cheryl

Welcome Home!

What does your tent look lIke?
Is it square, round or pyramid shaped?
Made of sticks, straw or bricks?

Some say---
Follow Us.
We are leading the Way.
Our camp is better, shinier.

I say---
We are all important--
No one group leads the way--
There are many groups in the Camp of Humanity.

I was told--
You don't understand---
You don't live the way we do.
You are a house dweller.

We may live in different structures
Some on wheels--
In trees--
or even underground--

Lets remember what it means to be human.

compassion, humility, dignity--
allowing , accepting and including--

We are all in the ship together.
This ship called Earth
is accelerating---

Soon,
she will reach the speed of light---
speed of thought---

She has invited us along for the journey.

How will we behave on the trip?
Will we fight with our fellow passengers?

Do we think we deserve a better seat---
First class?

Do we hold grudges,
blame others
for our circumstances---
past, present, future

Do we judge others as unworthy?
It's their own fault
they are where they are.

We each have been given
a 'seat' on this journey---

We can move at any time--
pivot
adjust
grow

Become more than our programming.
Unify.

We are the many
and we are One.

Welcome to the Camp of Humanity.

Threads by Cheryl

Aloha...Akua
Aloha...Akua

I will hold the line.
Be an anchor.
I Am holding hands
with the Divine.

---A lifeline has formed.

Grab on the kite string
don't let it fly away!

Be the golden thread---
The thread of change
Evolution

Slip thru
the eye of the needle.

We are One
of the many threads
in this tapestry of life.

All the Things You Do by Cody

All the things you do
Will come back to you
The delay is a protection
Be patient with your projections
Only masters can instantly precipitate
The rest of us have to wait
Its been years since my heart bell has rang
Long ago I put my love out there
Now its coming back like a boomerang

Full Circle by Cheryl

---Heart to Heart---

I want you back.
Return.
Become one again.

We are becoming.
Gaining
        Our power.

With great power
comes
Responsibility.

You are safe child---
they are your choices
that come back to you--

Back again---
How you treat others
comes back to you.

Full circle.

One Day You Will Fly Again
by Cody

Run crazy through freedoms tapestry
Appreciate our ancient mothers warm thread
Woven throughout time and space
Comforting as a lovers smile
Free as a child stomping in a rain puddle
Kick the leaves as you run through them
Notice the patterns they make
Where do your ripples on the water go
How many colors of eyes are there
What do the songs of birds mean
Oh how the plants love the songs
The rain, the sun
Shake the rain from your wings
One day you will fly again

Fly Free by Cheryl

Round and Round
We go

swirl, whirl, twirl

Take your turn.

I am the marble in the Roulette wheel---
Circling.

I am a pebble in the whirlpool.

Take your turn.

Turn dirt into pearls.

I Am a pearl.

Go thru the furnace---come out,
all shiny and new---
Phoenix.

Fly Free--
unencumbered by others ideas, expectations, demands.

"Don't throw your pearls to swine."

Ocean by Cheryl

The Monad,
the One---
the eternal point.

We are the descendants---
sons and daughters
of all that is.

We share consciousness---
coming from Source.

Return.
We become
by going inward.

Inside
there is a depth--
an ocean of consciousness--
sea of eternity.

Bloom Out of Sadness
by Cody

In a sea of changes.
Where uncertainty prevails.
Will we be the captain of discontentment?
Trying to dictate the outcome.
Abandoned and lost in the water spout illusion of the past.
Watching the endless production of disdain.
Playing out over and over in our mind.
Or will we awake in the only real time.
Open our heart to now.
Embrace our blessings.
Thank what we have.
See the ocean of possibilities for what they are.
Or keep having a tea party on a tossing ship.
A ship going in circles.
Party of mad man archetypes.
Fools convinced they've been fooled.
Castaways from the grace of goodness.
Spinning their wheels in the mud of ungratefulness.
Or open to gratitude.
Realize the cycles of change are the greatest gifts.
Freedom of will has got us here.
So far from the shore of the life we so dearly crave.
Freedom of will will guide us back.
Hope is a sure fire compass.
I will put the wind back in my sails.
Circumstance is an opportunity for innovation.
The blues are not sung by the royal.
The real songs of soul.
Written only from the awareness of those tried by fire.
Forged in the cauldrons of experience.
Unique as the waves that those their vessel about.
The balance of a tight rope walker.
Earned from the swing of uncertainty.
Trust that there is a much grander author.
The story you are in is bigger than your woes.
If you knew how wonderful you are.

You would be paralyzed with vanity.
Shine like a fire fly.
Dance in the dark.
Ride the cycle.
Arise to the dawn of your soul.
Sleep no more in the shadow of self torture.
Bloom in the sun of the gift of the world.
For you are the flower of God.
Planted and nourished by the sacred elements
Strengthened by the trails of time.
Dance in the wind of change.
You are the finest art of the ages.

Stupid Cupid Shooting his Arrows
by Cody

There you are at the top of your game.
Looking sharp as razor.
Fine as a silver cup.
Ducks in a row.
Bills paid.
Books read.
Research done.
Worries banished.
Hair styled.
Goals accomplished.
Peers impressed.
Art collected.
Pins placed perfectly on a map.
Prim and proper are your two best friends.
No need to be caught up in any risky romance.
X factor calculated.
Experience has led you to the lonely tower.
Safe from any risk.
Dust can't collect with your choir regiment.
Dream car in the drive way.
Prime residential estate.
Perfect location.
Bed is made as tight as a marines.
Run every day.
Work out routine in line.
Strict diet.
You get the drift before the news does.
Your prize roses are growing in your garden.
While your dreams are dying on the vine.
Happiness destroys routine.
Routine is the destroyer of happiness.
Is it not time to make the most beautiful of all mistakes?
A necessary risk we all must take.
Or be choked by what's necessary.
The most wonderful and risky mistake of them all.
The grandest and brave maneuver of all spiritual acrobatics.
There you go follower of the heart.
The world has no safety net.
For the Triple Lindy of life.
Best of luck.

19

May stupid cupid hit his target.
May you find the most blind phenomenon in the universe.
Make the biggest and best mistake there is.
LOVE. LOVE. LOVE.
STUPID CUPID SHOOTING HIS ARROWS.
LET YOUR LOVE LIGHT SHINE SO HIS CHANCE OF MISSING YOUR BIG
HEART NARROWS.

In-Between by Cheryl

What happens
'Between the Listening and the Telling'*?

Where does the healing magic happen?
Do we go somewhere else?
Elsewhere.
What else is there?

What do we become?
The becoming---
Listen and learn.
Remember.
Do you ever wonder?
Wander--about, around
life.
Hop, jump and skip
around,
Go on a walk about.

Round and Round we go.

*Mark Yaconelli

We Are Forever
by Cody

You cannot break what is not bound
It must be lost to be found
Run free my friend into your bliss
When you return I will greet you with a kiss
There is no upside without a down
The water itself cannot drown
My love is water
You are the sea
As infinite as space
You are part of me
I do not break rules
I see how much they can bend
Without walls there is nothing to defend
Run me over for a thousand lives
Marry me a million times
Throw me in the fire to be forged
Eat my flesh until your gorged
I will never be alone
We are forever, beyond the norm
I sense you in my heart though we are not together
A true love can weather any tether
I cut the cords and free each other
I call upon the universal judge and the divine mother
Free us from any contracts we have made
All its expectations that enslave
Bring us back our child like innocence
Cast away our adult learned ridiculousness
I will not beg I will command
The elements of this land
Free me from the pain I cause
I cast you out contracts and laws
Open my heart to endless love
For those who push will be shoved
Certain things have their place
Others must be let out of my cage
Wash me clean of this pain
I can hold it no further
Only love will remain, open and free is my true nature
I've came to learn from the earth, to me she caters
She loves me Unconditional with all my flaws
For I am her child although I'm lost

Some day I will be as wise as her
On that day she will take me back and all I've served
All I've done and all I haven't
All my good and bad habits
All I am and all I'm not
She loves beyond any plot
I love her back with all of my heart
I forgive my self and all my fault
For I am a gift from end to start
Now that I realize
We breathe art

Where Dreams Come True
by Cheryl

On the Merry-Go-Round of Life---
Up and Down,
Round and Round

Here we go---

Take a Leap--
Dive deep--

Hold your breath--
Squeeze your eyes--
shut tight--

Jump
down the wormhole---

To the rainbow
play with Peter Pan--
in Never Never Land.

On the Merry-Go-Round of Life---
I'm gonna ride
all nite long.

The strong wind blows--
to the rainbow--
where dreams come true.

Catch
the next train to Georgia---
Follow the birds
Fly south for the winter.

Past the smog--
You'll find a city in the sky--
Never Never Land
where dreams come true.

Have you lost your way?
Shut your eyes--
hold your breath--

Pull the plug
go down the drain.
Ride the wind

Round and Round
We go
On the Merry-Go-Round of Life.

The Birds Sing Morning Songs
by Cody

The birds sing morning songs
To the trees
To the water
To the air
They sing and love
No matter what the storm has done
If it ripped there nest apart
If the lightning struck and killed there love
They care not
Their song is an example of their unconditional support
My elderly woman friend is the same
She invites me to events whether I show or not
It is not her concern if I appear or disappear from her life
She loves me none the less
Like a child she sets a plate for
Supporting them even when they don't show
Others use there friendship like weapons
They wield the power imbalance like a knife
If you do this then you can have my attention They say
If you do this I will do that
Our friendship is a ship
I am captain of They say
They use their love as a weapon
A possession of control
This I must have done at some point
Everything around me is a reflection
I can't blame or hate them
For they are one of my aspects
A past less evolved me
Still they are me
Me showing me to myself
It's all creation
It's all evolution
Time is merely to organize progression
I must have boundaries
I show how I deserve and need to be treated
How can they know if I don't show
I am the example
Still I will treat them as I would want to be treated
A golden rule we all have to act on
Conditions are not love

Unconditional love and boundaries can be confusing
I'm tired of the ships of Conditions
We must all be our captains
When together we must agree to understand
To accept
To forgive
I see the my user self and how I control
I do have to pull back my reins of giving
Constantly ask myself
Is this truly to give
Is this to manipulate
A gift can take anothers power away
Contingent love is not love
A mother would never take her love from her child
Based on what they had done
It's an endless spring
It flows from her mountain of wisdom
She knows she does not own this wisdom
Therefore she gives it endlessly without Conditions
I love you my gem
My Ruby
My Diamond that can cut me or heal me
It's my choice
I love you Unconditional
Sometimes I must run into myself
I'm not running from you
I'm running from the battles
I'm laying down my weapons
I'm retreating to better understand
To process
I'll be over here loving you from a distance
Sometimes the best support is from a far
I will cheer you on from here
Your love is not weapon
My gifts are not a form of control
I am a bird singing to the beautiful forest that is you
You are trees of observation
Oh I wish to be a tree
My songs only confuse
That is me
This is us

We are a community
We are the trees
We are the birds
We are the storms
All is well
All is in progress
I love you
Even when you won't and can't love me
I see you even when you can't see me
It's ok when you don't understand
I really don't either
I follow the example of the elderly woman
I invite you to the future
The past is not my concern
If you show or not is not my concern
If I won't teach you who will
All is well between heaven and hell
My spine will be straight
My eyes will be open
My bed will be made
I will be here in the place I love
Drinking the sacred water
Breathing fresh air
I am never alone
I never will be
With or without you
The fire in my heart warms me
Good vibes your way
I forgive myself for my trespasses
I forgive you
I hope you can forgive me some day
I'm only a lower becoming evolved
I can't do it on my own
We all need each other
On our way home

Syllabus for Life by Cheryl

Grandmother says
"Young one,
Let me give you some advice---

Look forward---
Stay Focused.

Don't worry what others are doing---
Follow your own heart whispers."

Sometimes,
the way we think is ours---
is not. So,
find your way!

Be aware--
Everyone is doing their thing---
Don't compare!

Our job is to find
Our thing.

FOMO
Fear of Missing out---

Is the grass always greener
on the other side---

Feeling sorry--
Making comparisons--
Feeling left out--

"But they have it better than me."
"No one knows the troubles
I've seen."
29

Honey,
that's your path--
your contract
for your soul development.

Do you realize
you chose the details?

I Am
a tight rope walker---
balance beam gymnast---
Teetering between---
Compassion and Boundaries.

What happens if I fall?

I Am following my own Syllabus.

Can't worry about
what others are doing---

No longer concerned
about what I'm missing.

I know--
I Am here for my stuff.
What's for me--
comes my way.

My map is internal.
It is my Syllabus for Life!

Give Thanks by Cody

I'd like to thank my supporters out there. Seen and unseen.
Friends, family and teachers and students.
All the earth and its elements.
All the directions.
All the gods and devils.
The moving and the stagnant.
The numbers.
0s and 1s.
Spaces in between the solids.
The solids.
The plants.
All creatures alive and dead.
All ancestors.
All future beings.
All my past selves.
All my future selves.
All the roles I play and have option to play.
Above and below.
Fast and slow.
You get the point
I love and respect all spheres of turning.
All frequency felt and not felt.
I could go on.
I will go on thanks to all of us.
What a wonderful experience here in the hallway of infinite mirrors.
All my selves shattered.
We all will make it back together some day.
The spaces in between will be perfectly placed by the master composers.
We will all be the song of creation.
Thanks thanks thanks.
I'm so happy I can keep these lessons for now.
Some day I will let them go.

Treasure Hunt by Cheryl

Do you have a broken heart?

Rescue the shards of your heart.
They are treasure.

Search and Rescue.

What is hiding
down
In the
basement of your heart?

Go inward--
to the ward of your heart.

Go deep--dive
to the depths
of your soul.

Dive for treasure.
Treasure Hunt.

Go deep
into the
abyss of nothing.

Enter the Void--

The Black Hole
of complete emptiness.

Only then,
          can you
Run
with your wild horses.

Portal by Cheryl

Feeling gratitude and awe
for this next step.
We are on the cusp
of a Big Leap.

Who else feels it?
The excitement is in the knowing.
We have made it.
Give thanks to all your helpers.

I'm like a child's balloon filled with helium---
that needs held onto.
Catch it
Or,
let go--
Fly.

Slip thru the eye
of the needle.
Come out on the other side.
Portal.

Making Happiness Happen
by Cody

Is it that brand new out fit you wearing?
Did it make you smile?
The new gig you landed?
Another complete mile?
That fast car you drive?
Now you live, not just survive.
Out skipping in the sunshine.
Your face out of the pillow, where you hide.
Now you talking to your neighbors.
Calling up old friends.
Doing all the things you wanted to do.
You out playing again.
Is all this making you happy?
Laughing like a child.
Or is it you making it happy?
Bringing happiness all the while?
Oh how the world did miss you.
Yes indeed it did.
You are it's secret ingredient.
It was sad when you went and hid.
There is such extraordinary brightness.
When you shift your dial.
It was you all along making happiness.
Solely only you pulling it from the pile.
It's ok when you sing the blues.
We see when you put yourself on trial.
Just know the world is here for you.
Once you pardon yourself and walk down your isle.
When you realize you are your wealth.
Finally bury your own guilty file.
We have been waiting here for you patiently.
We sure did miss to see you smile.
The whole band has been practicing.
Oh how we do love your unique style.
So come out here and dance with us.
We're slipping on the tile.

We Are the Spice of Life
by Cheryl

Go to the park
and you will find---

a different composition
each and every day.

So much variety---
Variety is the spice of life.
We are the spice of life.

We all contribute to the mosaic---
the mandala, puzzle, picture.

We are creating a masterpiece---
Perhaps a new recipe---
for an award winning dish
the combination of those
11 secret spices---
which give the flavor
we are all craving.

Start with the water of life,
which flows from Earth's heart.
Take some pure love, grace and mercy
then add
the just right
amount of starlight (Tara).

In your Earthwalk
learn from mama squirrel---
always gathering, collecting--
even though she's busy
she takes time to say hello.

Those personal connections are necessary.

We are the many
and we are One.

We are the mosaic---
        the masterpiece
        the creation.

We are a meal
that nourishes each other.

Add your distinctiveness to the recipe.
Be part of the soup!
Your unique flavor is the missing ingredient.
We Are the Spice of Life!

Infinite Game of Hide and Seek
by Cody

You will find what you seek.
There is no hiding.
I knew it therefore it is.
So that's what I'm finding.
I definitely should not be holding.
Holding this magic wand.
I would never listen too.
Nor play this song.
Maybe I should stop.
Playing the blues.
It must be dictating.
The world that I choose.
I saw the real world.
In my dream last night.
Nothing was hidden.
Where all realities collide.
Nature was overgrowing.
The technological world.
Both were together.
In an infinite swirl.
I witnessed the beginning.
The creation of man.
The labs where the ape was altered.
By the alien's experimental hands.
Where they spliced gene number 2.
When they stirred the primordial soup.
Took the clay from the earth.
Created us from the goop.
Darwin was right excluding us.
Why is the question?
Make a monkey conscious.
All of this for what?
So we will see.
what's around.
Still not smart enough.
To respect its own ground.
The earth that we walk on.
Mother so strong.
Such a lovely creator.
We really don't belong.
Out of place in a time.

Pushing over the balance.
Maybe AI will find.
A solution for the challenge.
Oh it's so strange.
To go where I go.
To find what I seek.
To know what I know.
Through infinite dimensions.
I roam like a child.
The face of discovery.
So bright and wild.
I've truly seen the beginning.
From the witch we all came
The place we are going.
I will not name.
We go where we know.
So I will stay the course of the witness.
Hovering at the doorway of perception.
In order not to shift this.
This reality we are all riding.
Riding like a wave.
We must learn to swim.
If we are to be saved.
Be thankful for what we have.
Must be the mantra we sing.
Where we focus our minds.
Is the reality we are creating.
Who needs chains.
When the mind is enslaved.
Free yourself from your captors.
Before it's to late.
Your eyes are the window to your soul.
Stare in your mirror this moment don't wait.
Let go of your fears.
Open your gate.

Stockholm Syndrome
by Cheryl

Notice the word belief has a lie in it.
Believe the lie.
Live the lie.

There's a difference between
Knowing and Believing
----(Knowing is Divine)----
Belief is a system of control
a safety net.

We are being held captive
by belief systems.

Our beliefs are a trap
to control
our every thought and action.

Kidnapped.
Do you love your captor?
Stockholm Syndrome.

Our beliefs---
lies that hold us down.

Small human---
Dependent on--
Technology--
transportation, housing, food.
Systems--
economic, medical, governmental.
Systems of control.

Leave the lies of belief.
Become free.
Free of story, mind and body.

Free your soul.

The One Lesson by Cody

So I've pulled a few lessons out of my experience as a person living
life on earth.
I met God and the Devil
They are two sides of a sword
One is attached to outcome
One isn't
One wants to hold on to every experience and possession out of
fear of loosing it
One wants to let everything go free knowing that you have to let go
of everything one way or another
Not to receive but to truly clear and move on
In return that letting allows new experience people and possessions
to come into a person's life
When we hold on to anything be it a feeling, a possession, a
substance, a person or anything--
we are on the stagnant side of life and are in a state of hell
hence the devil side of the sword
A stuck place
A place of pain because we are not letting the energy out
When nothing goes out nothing can come in
To have true God like nature, Christ consciousness, I Am presence,
or how ever you want to put it--
we've got to realize this is not our possession or even part of us
Creation is infinite energy that can never be created or destroyed
Everything here on earth stays here in this closed loop system
It is not alive or dead
It just is
Basically there is a negative and positive charge in the universe
0s and 1s
Negative/Positive
It can be represented in all objects places people and things
Man woman and have some of both in each
Masculine and feminine
Light dark
Night day and so on
This allows movement
The Dow explains it best to me
True nature moves in cycles
We own nothing
It's all for learning
We have or we don't have for a short time

Everything is recorded forever
Everything has a memory
We will will play out every scenario from the beginning to the end
of time
It's all evolution to make things flow perfectly
We have been each other
We will be each other
It's all a role
We will all play each part until every tiny particle has been a king,
queen and so on
We all have a past and a future in this Earth
Basically all for one lesson
To learn how to let go
How to die Basically
How to truly give everything we possess
Because it's just that
This place uses our infinite ability to to exist
It needs us to exist
We don't need it
As infinite travelers we can go anywhere
It's not the going that is hard
It's letting go of what we think we need
It's trying to control out of fear that we will loose,
what we never had
what we can never have
Our cars
Our homes
Our trees
Our friends
Our whatever, ours nor ours
They are the earth's
They are creations
They are the idols
To worship any possession, experience, people, anything is to not
worship creation itself
Creation and destruction
Basically a beginning and an end
Everything here on earth has a beginning and an end
Souls do not
We are infinite
So basically realize all things and the experience will end
Don't try to hold on to anything
Love it
Experience it
Be kind to him and her

Grow with it then let it go
It really is just a passing of the sacred pipe that is all things
Problems lay in holding on
The devil means to hold on
Evil means to hold on
In some way it is to control the freedom of choice of another sacred object here on earth
Earth is a closed loop system
Nothing leaves here
If we are to make it out we must let go
If we are to have experience anything we must realize its just that
If if treats you bad treat it good
As you would want to be treated
There is no swine
Everything is deserving of your pearls
We will play every role
It's all to evolve and get better
It's all Ground Hog day
OK that's me out of the rabbit hole
It's been fun learning
I hope you get something out of this
It's been said before and it will be said again
Over and over until we all get it right
Perfection is possible
It just means there will be no more elements of holding on
All diseases come from cancer
Cancer holds on and tries to control the entire organism
The devil is cancer
The devil cancer, the freckle if you will as the great Josh Jerue put it,
Hold on and trust to control outcomes
God, Creation knows through lessons nothing is owned
Everything evolves if it is free to come and go at the time and place it needs to
It's birth it's death
All the rest
So let go what no longer serves you
At the same time nourish and respect what does serve you
Love it
Enjoy it
Honor it
It is using you as much as you are using it
It will one day let you go when it is done with you.
Let it go on its own free will
42

Holding on is hell
Honoring it's wishes is heavenly or god like
Gods know everything is infinite, free and forever
Devils, demons whatever you call them hold on
They are stuck here on earth forever
Always have been and always will
I love you
Hopefully someone reads this and understands
It can help them be free and happy and move on
Or realize what they have should be honored
To nourish what nourishes them
Some things, people, experiences, etc. should be honored, kept as long as it serves both parties
Others should end, the relationship and move on.
To each their own at their own time and place is what I say
Easy said sometimes difficult to do
Best of luck on your learning
Enjoy what you have while you have it
It's all for you as an individual
It's all for the collective growth and evolution of all souls.
Thanks Earth
Thanks God and Devil
You are both my friends
Both teachers
0 and 1
I love you
Thanks everyone and everything
that plays a role in my progress as a better whatever I am
I'm am that I am
I'm not not that I'm not

Authors---

Cody Ray Richardson lives in the Mount Shasta area. This is his first book of inspired poetry.

Cheryl Lunar Wind lives in the Mount Shasta area in a little town called Weed. She is a practicer of Mayan cosmology, Lakota ceremony, Star Knowledge and the Universal Laws including the Law of One. Her hobbies are writing poetry, music, dance, drum circles and love for all life; plant, animal and crystal. Cheryl has been a guide and spiritual teacher for many years. Now she shares wisdom and wit through poetry, and has published poetry books; Know Your Way, We Are One, Follow the White Rabbit, Love Your Light and LIFE: Shared thru Poetry.

Testimonials---

"Cheryl's poetry is very inspiring--particularly the way she compares life with the forces of nature. There is a special element in her poems that opens my heart and fills my soul with divine possibilities."
Giovanna Taormina, Co-Founder, One Circle Foundation

"Cheryl's poems have helped me to uncover and honor my own hidden memories. The beauty of her spirit is evident in each tender, insightful passage."
Marguerite Lorimer, www.earthalive.com

Made in the USA
Middletown, DE
02 July 2023